Auras, Clairvoyance and Psychic Development

Energy Fields and Reading People

2nd Edition

Crystal Muss

Table of Contents

Introduction

Since ancient times, people have been able to perceive an area of light above others' heads. This would go on to explain why most cave paintings and murals depict spiritually advanced beings having a halo around their heads. For example in Australia's remote Western Kimberley, one of its nine regions which is characterized by steep plateaus, prehistoric cave paintings of people have been depicted with golden haloes around their head. We can also see them in the depictions of many ancient Egyptian gods and goddesses such as Ra and Isis.

Long ago, when devout men and women were more preoccupied about their healthy existence rather than with desires which had a materialistic foundation, they could perceive these so-called auras with ease. It helped them become a good judge of character. Spiritual leaders like Jesus, Buddha, etc. were always depicted as having an aura around them. An aura is said to reflect a person's individuality and his or her core character.

For decades now, the field of science has come forth with proof of the existence of auras in varying different formats and experiments. There have been eyewear devices invented to help facilitate the viewing of these auras and explanations as to how they are generated. And although the efforts of science assist those who are not readily willing to accept the existence of such things as auras beyond the reality we take for granted and really know so little about, all of us possess the ability to experience this seemingly phantom glow for ourselves naturally.

From the mystic to the scientific, we will explore the nature of auras, their characteristics, purpose, and benefits in this book. You will come to better understand why each of us feels the presence of our own personal bubble and learn how we can maintain a healthy sense of it. You will also be provided with various techniques on learning how to view auras for yourself so that you may become adept at reading people with practice. So let us start our journey to understand Auras and how they can affect our lives.

Chapter 1: What is an Aura?

Every object and organism in the universe is surrounded by an electromagnetic field in its immediate vicinity. An aura is an electromagnetic field that surrounds a human being. This energy field is sometimes referred to as a Human Energy Field (HEF). This is how most people think of auras, but each living thing from animals to plants and non-living things such as crystals and gems have auras too. The nature of these auras simply varies from person to organism to inanimate object.

There are two main views on the origins of auras that can be found in both the scientific and spiritual communities, and really they are both just looking at the same thing from different perspectives. One view holds that auras emanate from the cellular and electrochemical activities going on within our bodies to create this electromagnetic field. The other view sees the aura as an energetic representation of our true selves and has more to do with determining the mental, emotional and physical states of our being rather than the other way around. It is a bit like the chicken and the egg argument to summarize, depending on your understanding of the universe, but for simplicity's sake and the salvation of length for this book, we can say that the aura and everything else that compiles our existence – be it a mindset, physical body, emotions and consciousness – are all intimately connected.

The principle that becomes the focal point of both views mentioned above has to do with vibrations. We are talking about atomic and subatomic vibrations and their frequencies, the varying frequencies of waves on the electromagnetic spectrum and waves of light both visible and invisible. In this sense, every single thing in this universe has a vibration; from the densest rock to the Earth itself, to people, to water, to what is real and quite literally what is imaginary as well. Different thoughts carry vibrations and so do emotions. Sounds are easy to comprehend as carrying vibration, and the difference in frequencies of all these things have different effects on us whether we are aware of them or not.

Without getting too technical, if you remember from your high school physics class, almost everything is made of atoms, or particles, which are constantly in motion. Solid objects have particles that are packed in very closely together and vibrate off one another. Liquid particles have a bit more room to move around and can slide past each other, which give liquids their particular properties as matter. Gas particles have even more room than solids and liquids to bounce around. One type of medium is allowed to pass through another as long as that second medium has more space between their particles. This is why dense solid objects can sink and move through water and both solids and liquids can pass through a gaseous environment, which is pretty much everything under the sun in our atmosphere. Solid objects that float on water do so because there are pockets trapped in them that contain gas, such as the case for most wood and rocks like the pumice stone.

Waves and rays such as the radio, micro and UV variety behave differently in that they are not exactly matter, rather they are concentrations of energy that can be beamed through the space between particles. This is why you can receive radio wave signals inside your house and why there is talk about radio wave signals being beamed out into space. Light, whether visible in the spectrum of the rainbow or invisible on the ends of the spectrum from infrared to UV, has been proven to behave as both a wave and a particle simultaneously. This makes it a different kind of animal altogether. It can pass through gases, liquids, and solids such as glass and crystal prisms and changes its course of direction depending on the medium. Consider going to a laser show sometime and you will get a better idea of what I mean. Light follows a simple rule though, which is to travel the path of least resistance.

Now when it comes to fields, these are three-dimensional spaces which have an intensity of charged particles that changes or diminishes as they move further away from their source. An electromagnetic field is one that is created from running electricity through a medium, influencing the particles around it. If you think of any type of wire in your house or one connected to an electronic device, what is happening to transmit that power is that highly charged ions cause the atoms of the metal wire to send other charged ions down the line. When this happens, the electric ions affect the metal atoms in such a way that they give off a field of charged magnetism around the wire, even though the insulated covering.

Every type of electronic device creates these fields. If you remember for the first few years when cell phones hit the mainstream market there was concern about the radiation coming off of them causing adverse effects to people's health, mostly in the form of cancerous tumors. While the effect of these devices has shown not to cause such immediate and detrimental problems, their continual use over longer periods of time still do influence our bodies and minds. If you have ever been to a music concert where a musician brings their plugged in electrical instrument too close to the amplifier, you will know that unforgettable high-pitched whine that is caused by the distortion of contrasting electromagnetic fields.

A similar thing happens to us by constantly being in the direct vicinity of electronic devices on subtler levels. This is why it is recommended to keep cell phones away from your person as much as possible, carrying them in a bag instead of your pocket for example. It is also recommended to keep alarm clocks and computers as far away from your bed at night as possible, at least three feet in distance, especially from your head.

Now, if you have ever heard of certain crystals, stones and gems having healing properties for living organisms, it is due to the auric field that they emit. They can be used for a multitude of purposes depending on the properties of the crystals and stones themselves, from personal energetic healing and promotion of mental clarity to cleansing the space in a room and holding a certain vibration beneficial to anyone who enters. I was skeptical of this notion myself at first, but there is a very practical and scientific explanation behind it.

Each crystal and stone has a percentage of silica in it that, based on the quantity and structure, holds a vibration that has a direct influence on the minerals and other components of our bodies. If we are ill or experiencing an energetic block of some sort, the aura of these crystals and stones – the vibrational field that they emit – interacts with our own aura and silica composition in our bodies, raising a low vibration of ill health to higher vibrations, promoting a sense of healing.

Think about it: every electronic device we know of today contains a quartz crystal or some variant in its hardware. The ideal structures of these crystals streamline the power and function of these devices. Watches contain quartz crystals as well to maintain their steady pace. The difference in the auras of these crystals and stones as opposed to living organisms is that they do not fluctuate – they remain fixed.

Only when a person places their conscious intentions into these inanimate objects does their auric output increase. Or when used excessively for healing purposes, the output of the crystals and stones decreases and they require cleansing. Once a conscious influence has been removed from these crystals and stones, their output remains fixed again. We will further discuss the influence of consciousness on auras later in the chapters on detecting and observing auras as well as auras in healthcare.

Let's take a look at the human composite. Now that we have discussed the fundamental principles of vibrations and electromagnetic fields, you will have a better idea of the inner workings in how the auras of living organisms work and what they actually are. From the standpoint of our bodies' physiology and our emotions determining the nature of our auras, let's first take a look at the network of neurons running throughout our bodies. Neurons are the cells that allow every other single cell in the body to speak to each other. They create a vast network in the brain and travel down the brainstem down the spine as the spinal cord, branching out to different places in the body. They connect to our organs and muscles to help regulate the body's metabolic processes, hormone levels, and response and reaction to external stimuli.

Although the firing of neurons to send signals throughout the body is chemically induced, it is the electrical impulses of these neurons that carry the messages throughout vast lengths in the body from the brain to the body and vice versa. You can consider the electrical firing of these neurons to act similarly to the wires carrying electricity that we discussed earlier. Some neurons are insulated, some are not, but they nonetheless create a field around them that can interact with other minerals and metals in the body such as iron in the blood pertaining to hemoglobin – that which allows blood to transport oxygen throughout the body to cells for healthy function. They also affect the percentage of water in the body, which we will discuss a little later.

Exploring this further, we must take into consideration where people predominantly place their attention in their lives to better understand their aura type. This will incorporate the Eastern energetic systems of the chakras and meridians that flow throughout the body. For example if a person is primarily focused on materialistic gains and losses or predominantly athletic or focused on the body, their attention leans to the root of the chakra system at the base of the spine. Most of their activity will be centered on this area, inciting greater neural activity here, which is associated with the color red. Therefore a person who is mainly focused on these physical aspects of life will exude a red aura.

Similarly, if a person is a great communicator and excels in speech, making it a core part of their daily lives, their attention will be focused toward the throat, which is associated with the color blue and will result in their having a blue aura. One more example would be a pensive person who mostly uses their brain to approach the demands of life with their thinking skills. They might have great insight into situations where others do not, and so the majority of their neural activity will be centered at the third eye chakra which is associated with the color indigo, and thus they will give off an indigo colored aura.

This goes to show that where we direct our attention plays a major role in determining the nature of our aura. Indeed, linking with the level of consciousness or awareness we exert in our lives greatly affects the way our auras manifest. I had mentioned before that our thoughts and emotions carry vibrations. To illustrate a brief demonstration of this principal, have you ever noticed someone being angry, sad, or joyous without them blatantly expressing it? There may be clues such as body language present, but if you are able to feel it coming off of them without a verbal or physical cue, you are subsequently walking right into their auric field without realizing it.

This field has varying densities because the electromagnetic waves vary with densities as the waves permeate through the physical matter of a living being. In humans an aura is known to define a radius of almost two to three feet around them, or about an arm's length. This area or span of an aura is known as the "auric egg". The measurement of an arm's length is an average estimation of the size of an aura, however this area can fluctuate depending on the conscious, emotional and physical factors that a person is experiencing at the time. An aura can withdraw to the surface of the skin at various particular places on the body or all around, or it can expand in all directions, including into the ground and through walls, to twice the size of the average radius. As a person expands their consciousness in spiritual practice, the size of their aura naturally expands as well. The aura is sometimes seen as a flow of personal energy around the body.

Our Personal Bubbles

We are constantly being bombarded by all kinds of electromagnetic waves in our environment. We are influenced by those emitted from cell phone towers, power lines, electronic devices and so on, and by considerably more sources when living in cities. Likewise, we are constantly coming into contact with the influence of other people's auras. When someone walks by close to you, you may feel as if he or she has siphoned off some of your energy. At other times, a sudden grasp of your arm might seem like an intrusion of your privacy.

Have you ever walked into a room of people and felt a sudden change within yourself without good reason? It may feel like they were having a private conversation and felt intruded upon, or you just walked into a space of high energy that suddenly causes you to feel overwhelmed or even right at home, depending on who you are.

When surrounded by a set of people, sometimes you might naturally feel the need to move away from them. Or when perusing a public place, you might feel inexplicably drawn to a certain enigmatic person just to be around them or engage them. Have you ever felt extremely comfortable in the company of a person without knowing them too long? It is because they are giving off a very calm and soothing "vibe" – now no longer a slang term since we have a better understanding of the effects of vibrations. These subconscious reflexes indicate the presence of an aura and the ability of the human consciousness to sense it.

Have you ever noticed that someone you are unfamiliar with may step in range of you closer than you are comfortable with, while you allow friends and family to get closer to you? There is an interesting phenomenon that people most often naturally abide by when it comes to the familiarity level of a relationship which speaks further to the subconscious sense of our auras with regard to personal space.

When people are first meeting each other or have become acquaintances, they will normally stand about six feet apart from each other in conversation. This is the distance in which they are each comfortable in their own personal space where their auric fields, normally about a three-foot radius from the body, are free from influence of the other or are just touching to get a sense of the other.

As a relationship develops and two people become friends, the increasing comfort level of familiarity and being around each other usually sees the diminishing physical space between them when spending time together. Typically at this level, friends will be about three feet away from each other when talking or hanging out. Each has gotten a sense of what it is like to be in the other's vicinity – their auric field – and allow themselves to share each other's space equally.

In the case of best friends, close family members and intimate partners, people will know the feeling of what it is like to be directly in that person's field so well that it is a shared comfort and they draw closely to each other, within one to two feet, on a regular basis where direct contact (causal touching) is commonplace and welcome.

Significance of an Aura

The colors and varying intensities of an aura have their own meanings. They are unique to a person and cannot be forged. It's almost similar to a person's tell when playing poker, if you are familiar with the expression. Each person's aura becomes a unique signature unto him or herself and reveals certain characteristics about that person. Reading auras is very similar to and perhaps the cornerstone for all mind-reading activities. As you develop your skills at reading auras to advanced levels, you will find that the amount of information you can interpret from them becomes very in-depth.

Becoming proficient at reading and sensing auras comes with many benefits, as it is a practice of developing another sense of yours just like you might acquire benefits from honing your eyesight or sense of hearing. In this case, since developing your ability to sense auras involves expanding your consciousness to better understand the world around you, you will come to know yourself better as well as others on many levels.

You will come to know that the quality and characteristic of a person's aura tells many things about them that might not be readily apparent just from inferencing information in a conversation. Getting a sense of a person's aura will help you to understand their true intentions as well as more about their personality. In accordance with reading auras and applying the information you know about them, you will be able to get a better sense of what kind of environment you are in around people.

This quality is especially beneficial to empaths, or people who are very sensitive to the emotional state of others around them. Oftentimes empaths endure added stress in life because they are picking up other's emotions whether they are aware of it or not and feel those emotions themselves which can be taxing on their energy and confusing as to where the emotions are coming from and how to deal with them properly. Reading auras will allow these sensitive people to become more aware of the source of these emotions so they can know not to take them on as their own, and even learn how to properly protect themselves against those who project or gush unhealthy emotional vibrations around them.

In recognizing the traits of another person's aura, you

can also develop a better sense of how to engage and relate to that person. For example, a person with an orange aura tends to be particularly creative, so getting involved with them in collaborative projects is a great platform to connect and bring out the best in them. If you notice a dim aura in a person or grey or black patches, you know that this person is unhealthy and you will be able to make a better decision about whether to avoid them or ask questions specific to the area to bring it to their attention in a compassionate way, and you may even offer to aid in healing them for that aspect if you feel that is a part of your calling in life.

Observing a person's aura enables you to read their thoughts before they say it out loud or even refrain from saying it altogether, but it helps to keep an objective point of view – that is, non-judgmental – when doing so. If an aura does not agree with what he or she is saying then you can confirm that the person is lying. Auras are natural and cannot be faked, even if the person is lying. In simple terms, a person with a bright, clear aura can be regarded as one who is pure and of good intentions while a dark and muddy aura may be indicative of unclear intentions or scheming. So then as you become proficient at maintaining the view of a person's aura while speaking to them, if they are consciously aware of telling you something that is false, you will notice their aura begin to dim or get dull.

Children are considered to be adept at reading auras. This would explain why infants tend to stare into the space above a person's head. A dark aura seems to upset them regardless of however nice he or she might seem in person. Children usually exhibit cleaner and stronger auras. They are not tainted by the materialistic world where we are forced to subdue our nature and assume a less than genuine personality. Kids who are now just entering their teenage years are aware and accept that they were able to see auras at one point of time when they were younger. This talent fades away as the child grows due to a lack of proper training.

Chapter 2: Aura Colors and Their Meanings

Red

A red colored aura relates to anything and everything concerned with the physical body. To be more specific, it also concerns the heart and circulation. As the densest color in the spectrum, red is known to create a lot of friction. It is highly unstable and can attract or repel at the same time.

On the negative side it may represent obsessions or financial problems; bottled-up anger and a vengeful capacity against forgiveness. It is commonly associated with anxiety and nervousness too. A person having an aura of a deep red nature can be expected to be grounded and realistic. This person is active and blessed with strong will power.

Such a person can survive in any kind of situation he or she might find themselves in. A muddied red color on the other hand, sends out one clear message; it portrays anger of a very repelling sort. A clear red color is one of the most sought after auras in a person. It signifies power and energy. These people are usually extremely competitive, sexual and passionate about everything they do. In its bright red state, red energy depicts an extremely healthy ego.

Pink

A pink colored aura personifies very loving, sensitive and tender characteristics. Such people are born artists. They are also known for their affection, purity and sensuality. A dark and murky pink depicts qualities that would put the bright pink auras to shame. It indicates that a person is immature and mostly of a dishonest disposition.

Orange

Orange is the color that is directly related to reproductive organs and emotions. It stands for vitality, vigor, excitement and loads of good health. Orange auras shout out the presence of a lot of energy and stamina. Such people are usually productive, creative and adventurous. They are known for being courageous and have a very outgoing social nature. A real time analysis could also indicate that they are currently experiencing stress due to appetites and addictions.

An orangey-red aura exudes a lot of confidence and

creative power. An orange-yellow person is extremely creative and intelligent. This person is a perfectionist and all of their work pays a very strict attention to detail. Hinting at a scientific background would not be very far from the truth.

Yellow

Yellow is always associated with the energy of life. It stands for inspiration and intelligence. It is an eye-opener type of aura. People with a yellow aura are usually easy going, creative, playful and extremely optimistic. Although it is very similar to the color yellow, a light or pale yellow denotes spiritual awareness and an emerging psychic. It also portrays hopefulness and optimism, especially an extremely optimistic excitement regarding new ideas. A bright lemon yellow color depicts a struggle to balance control and power in a business or personal relationship. It also portrays a fear of losing prestige, control, power and respect.

An aura that has a clear, shiny and bright gold metallic color shows that the person houses spiritual energy and power. This is a person who is very clearly inspired. A dark brown yellow or gold almost always points to a student or more specifically, someone who is putting a lot of effort into studying. A student trying to cram by making up for all the lost time, trying to study everything on the eve of an exam would be a perfect example.

Green

Green is a very soothing color, even as an aura. It pertains to the heart and the lungs. All of us see it as the color of everything healthy. It is a comfortable hue that is always associated with nature. This aura represents balance and growth. It symbolizes the love of people, nature and other social work. A bright emerald green is seldom associated with anything other than a healer or a person who is centered on love. A yellowish green aura is indicative of a person who is very communicative and creative at heart.

The most ominous green aura would be the dark or muddy forest green. It usually accompanies people who feel like they are victims of the world. Such people are prone to blame themselves or others constantly. They are consistently plagued with insecurity and low self-esteem. They are also extra sensitive and not very broad minded about criticism. Jealousy and resentment are also common ailments faced by them.

Blue

A blue color relates to the throat and thyroid. A person having an aura of this color is always cool, calm and collected. Their other character traits include having a caring or loving tendency. They are also remembered for being sensitive and intuitive. A turquoise aura always relates to the immune system. Such people are sensitive and compassionate. They are renowned healers or therapists.

A soft blue aura depicts peacefulness, honesty and an intuitive nature. Such people are also known for their communication skills. Clairvoyance, generosity and a high spirituality are synonymous with a bright royal blue color. These people are almost always on the right path by default. New opportunities are always in store for them. A dark or muddy blue color brings out the fears that are most dominant in a person. Most specifically is a fear of the future, fear of speaking or facing the truth and an underlying fear of self-expression.

Violet

A violet color is directly associated with the crown of the head, the nervous system and the pineal gland. It is regarded as the wisest and most sensitive of colors. It unearths the psychic power of attunement with oneself. The ones with this aura are usually idealistic, magical, artistic and intuitive. They are regarded as visionaries. Not very far from violet, the indigo aura has indicated a direct connection to the third eye, pituitary and visual gland. A lavender aura relates directly to the imagination and those who are daydreamers.

Silver

This is the color that stands for abundance, in both the spiritual and physical sense of the word. An abundance of bright silver can either be a cornucopia of wealth or a spiritual awakening. Bright, metallic silver corresponds that the person is receptive to new ideas. He or she could have a nurturing personality and could be extremely intuitive.

Gray

If gray clusters are seen in various parts of the body, it should be taken as a warning sign. It may be indicative of potential health problems. A muddy and darker gray color refers to the presence of a residue of fears accumulated in the body.

Gold

Gold is almost always considered to have a divine connection. It is regarded as the hue of enlightenment and celestial protection. A person with a golden aura is considered to have divine guidance. It is also associated with knowledge, wisdom, protection and spirituality.

Black

A black aura has the similar effect of a black hole. It transforms energy by drawing energy toward itself. It can be seen as capturing light and consuming it. It is also indicative of a darker past dominated by a tendency to harbor long-term grudges. If concentrated in one part of the body, this aura can be a signal to potential health problems.

White

As in real life, white is a pure state of luminescence. Most undefined regions in an aura are usually white. A white aura enables us to read spiritual, transcendent and etheric qualities in a person. It also represents truth and purity. Generally, white denotes angelic qualities. Sparkles or flashes of white color may say that angels are nearby or can shed light on an impending pregnancy.

Earth colors have only one true purpose. They represent an undying love for the earth. These colors are very important for a person. They are mostly seen in villagers and also in people who spend a lot of time outdoors. Rainbow colors point out that the person in question has just begun his or her first incarnation on earth. Pastels show a profound appreciation for serenity. A dirty brown overlay is known for holding on to energies and a lot of insecurities. A dirty gray overlay is indicative of energy blocks and stands for guardedness.

Chapter 3: Detecting and Observing Auras

Who is able to see auras? We have talked about children having the natural ability to do so and perhaps we hear about psychics and clairvoyants who possess this skill. The truth is that we are all able to see auras, it is inherent in our nature and we never lose the ability, but we must train ourselves if we want to get better at it. So why are some people more attuned to seeing and interpreting auras than others? There is the belief that it has to do with people's natural talents. Just as there are those who are naturally gifted at sports or musical instruments, some people are likewise gifted with this talent. There is also the belief that some people are more skillful at reading auras because they are visual learners as opposed to audio or kinesthetic learners.

There has been an argument from scientists who are more focused on the physical aspect of the human composite and their auras that aura detection and changes in the auras are related to external factors like humidity and temperature. Although, it has been suggested that the stasis of an aura will change in a person before the thought or emotion occurs that is related to the alteration. Studies conducted in Russia and presented in 2001 show that a thought appears in the aura before any electrical activity can be detected in the brain. This goes on to imply that consciousness is the most powerful resource we have in influencing everything from the state of our physical bodies to emotional balance and the nature of our thoughts to how we perceive our external environment and influence it as well. Studies in the power of consciousness and intention have been conducted over several decades and in a range of fields from bioenergy to psychology and psychotherapy, all producing fascinating results. We have talked before about how thoughts and emotions carry their own vibration, whether they are real or imaginary. Positive thoughts and emotions will always promote health, the expansion of consciousness, and enable the availability of opportunities. They carry a higher frequency (vibration), which can be related to electro-photonic vibrations we have been talking about. Negative thoughts and emotions will always depreciate health, confine a sense of awareness and limit the appearance of opportunity. These are of a lower vibration and cause distortion in the harmony of the natural world and our wellbeing.

I will tell you now that using these tools of positive intentions and affirmations has been proven to have a direct effect on our health, stimulating and increasing the strength of our auras, however I will reserve further details of this for the chapter on auras in healthcare. Instead, to further explain the influence of intentional consciousness in detecting and observing auras, we will take a look at the nature of water.

Water is considered to be inanimate, although it has been proven to hold memory along with maintaining a frequency based on the influence of its direct environment. In this way it acts the same as the crystals and stones that we spoke of earlier – its vibration remains fixed unless changed by someone's conscious effort. Now, designing a filtration system to purify water that would result in its holding a higher vibration can be considered a conscious effort, but we are talking about using thought and words directed on water to physically change its structure (purification or contamination), thereby increasing or decreasing its vitality, depending on the nature of the thoughts and words.

I have also said that water holds memory. I first learned this from a friend and experienced plumber who told me that there are only two things I need to know about water – the first is that it always flows down, the second that it retains memory. Try the following experiment and see for yourself. Plug a sink and fill it with water, then pull the plug and allow the water to drain out. Make a note of which direction the water swirls as it drains, either clockwise or counterclockwise. Plug the sink again and fill it up with water once more. This time when you pull the plug, put your hand in and swirl the water in the opposite direction you noted it going from before. Now that the water has drained, plug the sink and fill it one last time. This time when you allow it to drain, observe which direction it swirls. You will see that it is now going in the direction you had intentionally swirled the last full sink from before!

Masaru Emoto, a Japanese author, international researcher and entrepreneur, greatly contributed to the understanding of the effect of positive human consciousness (the influence of higher electromagnetic frequencies) through extensive research and experiments conducted on water molecules in the 1990s. The basis of his experiments involved saying good words, thoughts and prayers, and expressing love and joy to some containers of water and saying bad words, insults and expressing anger and hate to other containers of water. He would then freeze or crystalize these water molecules and view them under a microscope. The water that he expressed love and positive words to resulted in some of the most intricate and beautiful crystalline patterns like that of snowflakes. The water that he expressed hate and negative words to resulted in looking like corroded metal full of craters and holes. Remember this when considering that our bodies are comprised of more than 70% of water.

Semion Kirlian conducted research since the 1930s on the electro-photonic glow of an object (the electromagnetic field of a living or inanimate object, or an aura) in response to excitation in a pulsed electrical field. The extent of the excitation from the electrical field (created within a glass electrode) is adjusted to elicit the response of the object (your finger, for example) in the gas surrounding it (the air around your finger) so that it can be observed as a visible glow.

This principle, known as the avalanche effect, was first observed by Nikola Tesla in the late 1800s, but was named after Kirlian for his extensive research. To get a better visualization of this, think of those static electricity lamps surrounded by glass from the 1980s which emit a static electrical current to your fingers when you touch the glass, except the source of this electro-photonic glow pertaining to the Kirlian effect is coming from you instead. This observable visual is a representation of the specific electromagnetic field or aura that can be recorded for any given thing.

Professor K. Korotkov of St. Petersburg, Russia, is a leading scientist in this field of study regarding what is known as Kirlian Aura imaging. Using the same or similar method described above, Korotkov has provided imaging of the Kirlian Aura for two normal drops of water which are nearly identical except for one difference. While one water drop remained unaltered, the other drop was charged by a healer for ten minutes of him focusing his consciousness on that drop. The difference in the recorded auric vibrations of the two drops is astounding: the charged water drop showed an increase in vibration or auric size by more than 30 times that of the one that was left alone. Not only that, the physical and biological properties of the charged drop were observed to have been significantly changed as well. This may lend some insight as to why some religions practice blessing water and calling it Holy.

Aura layers

Auras are specific atmospheres surrounding people. Scientifically, they are made of electro-photonic vibrations which are generated as a reflex to some sort of external stimuli or excitation, as we have seen with the Kirlian effect. They are partly composed of electromagnetic (EM) radiation. The frequency of this radiation varies from infrared and micro waves on the low frequency band to ultra violet or UV light on the high frequency band.

The aura is a personal magnetic field that stretches to about two to three feet on all sides in a healthy and balanced person. The low frequency part of the spectrum seen in microwaves and infrared waves (body heat) has been theorized to be related to low levels of body function such as DNA structure, metabolism and circulation whereas higher frequencies like UV light are closer related to our conscious activity like thinking and decision making, creativity, intentions and emotions. We will see more evidence of this in the discussion of understandings coming from Reiki practices later on in the book.

Each aura consists of seven layers. These are said to be linked directly to the seven chakras present in the human body. The science behind an aura states that it consists of seven levels or auric bodies. These seven levels may be of varying densities and hues. Sometimes they may even be stark contrasts while some people might have monotonous auric eggs. Each auric layer has its own genuine frequency. They are interconnected and have an influence on each other. They also speak to the person's health, behavior, thinking, emotions and feelings. A slight variation in one of the bodies does have a considerable change on the other auras.

Each level possesses its own unique frequency and has an effect on the other levels around it. An imbalance in one level can lead to a corresponding imbalance in the other levels. The seven levels are as follows:

- **Physical level**: This level imparts information concerning the physical status of a person, i.e. what kind of physical backup he or she might need. Reading this aura successfully can help you determine if the person expects pleasure, comfort or health.
- **Etheric level**: This level is very simple to analyze. It has only two known meanings. At this level, the subject requires self-love and self-acceptance. It is important to make sure that self-esteem does not take a dip as far as this level is concerned.
- **Vital level**: As the name suggests, this level requires some clear thinking. It is paramount to comprehend situations in a clean, rational and linear way.
- **Astral level**: This layer is an indicator that the person requires some loving interaction and quality time with friends and family.

- **Lower mental level**: This level requires one to portray, speak and follow the truth.
- **Higher mental level**: This level insists that you have some kind of divine love. You must also have experienced spiritual ecstasy.
- **Spiritual (intuitive) level:** At this level, a comprehensive knowledge of the greater universal pattern and a link to the divine mind is required.

The best way for a beginner to start observing auras is to start sensing them. This means that you are expected to pay more attention when in someone's company. Inhale deeply, relax and redirect all you attention towards the physical condition of your body and your instincts. Colors that people have an affinity toward such as the clothing a person wears most often usually point to what color aura one resonates.

Analyze how that particular person makes you feel and think about which color aura would be ideal for such a person. With practice, sensing and seeing auras should become an easy affair, however when it comes to the layers, it will be difficult at first to see the higher ones. You must start with the first layer which emanates about one to two inches from the body. After getting comfortable with this, move on to the second one and repeat the same process, and so on through each layer. Another important tool required to see auras is to improve your peripheral vision. Our peripheral vision is relatively more functional than the central part of our retina. It has healthier photosensitive cells.

The reason behind the higher function of peripheral photosensitive cells and peripheral vision has to do with the way we have been trained all our lives to use our eyes in the way we see. All our lives in most every part of the world, we have been taught to use the central part of our retinas to focus on what is directly ahead of us. It is so ingrained in us that it becomes a perspective of life – look to the future, plan ahead, have an idea of where you will be in five years, etc. Often though this type of mentality causes us to forget and appreciate all the subtle nuances that happen in the present that are ripe with opportunity for us to grow in every direction and take advantage of the marvels that life has to offer.

Similarly, focusing on using the central part of our retina to see in our lives causes us to forget how to use our peripheral vision and take into reality all the natural phenomenon that occurs beyond the immediate physical realm. This is why children who are so adept at seeing auras at young ages lose that ability over time. With prolonged use of the central part of our retinas, the strength of our sight becomes exhausted and diminishes as we age. This is compounded by staring at artificially lit screens that are constantly in our faces like television, computers, and smartphones. Our eyes become used to looking at objects in a fixed way and a narrow distance. So that which allow us to see things from right up close to far off in the distance and every space in between along with panning in a wide scope for a greater range of vision - the flexibility of the lenses of our eyes – they too become fixed and harden with time, impairing our sight.

Improving your vision

With prolonged use in specific ways over the decades it can be tedious to view auras now. This can be remedied to some extent by following a few simple, rigorous exercises.

One exercise comes from the Yoga system that trains us to exercises the muscles attached to our eyes. The principle behind it is to improve circulation and health in our eyes so they are well-nourished and more relaxed, effectively reducing eyestrain. It takes about three to four minutes to do and can be done during anytime of the day, although it is recommended to do as soon as you wake up. Start by sitting up comfortably and breathing regularly with your eyes closed. Open your eyes and proceed to look up and then down six times. Follow by looking from the left to the right (or right to left) six times. Then look from the upper left corner of your eyes to the opposite lower right corner of your eyes six times, and the upper right corner to the opposite lower left corner six times. Finish by following a rotation of rolling your eyes clockwise six times and then counterclockwise six times. Close your eyes again and allow them to rest a little while. Repeat this entire set three times.

Another of these is known as the Qi Gong eye exercise. It involves adjusting your focus from near distances to far distances that will promote the flexibility of the lenses of your eyes and help maintain a good balance of near vision with far vision. Stand or sit with your arms extended straight out at your sides. Bending your arms at the shoulders and elbows and then the wrists, hold them out in front of you so that it feels like you are holding a big invisible ball in front of you with your palms facing you. You will want your fingers to be directly in your line of vision. Now part your fingers between the middle and ring finger, or the index and middle finger if the first is difficult for you, wide enough so that you can see between them. Practice focusing your eyes by looking in front of your hands and then between the spaces you have created with your fingers into the distance. Go back and forth in focusing your eyes like this for about ten times.

Now that you have a few exercises to improve the health of your eyes and central vision, let's take a look at regaining strength in your peripheral vision to see auras. Practicing using your peripherals is all about relaxing into it. If you find that you are trying hard at it or straining your eyes, you need to adjust your approach. We are talking about softening the gaze, so take your time and relax as you practice this.

Find a place that has a plain background (preferably white in color since it is the easiest to work with) such as a wall or a flat cloth curtain, or a large poster board. Make sure that the space you have chosen is softly lit. Start on seeing your own aura to begin with because you will always be with you and you can take as long as you need for this exercise without having to rely on the patience of another person. Hold your hand as far as you can up against the plain background with the back of your hand facing you and focus on the center of it.

While your eyes are directed at the center of your hand, begin to soften your gaze. Imagine your eyes getting sleepy but do not close them. Then without moving your eyes, direct your attention to the outline of your fingers.

Take as long as is needed, and you should begin to notice a faint haziness or kind of transparency just beyond the outline of your fingers. Move them together and then slowly spread them apart so there is just a little space between them. This movement will sometimes help you to catch the aura. Once you have caught a glimpse of a transparency or haziness around or between the space of your fingers, stop the movement and do not look directly at it, but increase your peripheral focus to help bring what you are seeing into clearer view. This haziness is your aura. With time and perhaps more practice as needed, you will start to notice this haziness take on a certain color as well.

Another training exercise to try by yourself is to look into a mirror, preferably a stationary one. Start by focusing on your nose with a relaxed gaze, not looking directly at the nose, but relaxing the gaze to view a half inch to an inch around the shoulders and head where a transparent haziness may appear. Have you ever been outside on a hot day and seen the heat waves rising up from the sidewalk or the street to make parts of it appear blurry? This is the kind of haziness that you should be looking for. If you are having trouble seeing it from using the nose, gently shift your gaze up to the center your forehead. Sometimes just that slight shift will help you pick up on the aura for the first time.

Again, stop the movement once you have caught on to your aura and increase your peripheral focus while still directing your eyes at your nose or forehead by putting your attention on the haziness about an inch beyond the outline of your shoulders and head.

With all this practice in newfound focus, you may find yourself drawn to take away your central gaze and look directly at your aura once you have found it, and then see that it disappears. That is ok! Reset your centralized focus, soften your gaze again, and direct your attention back to your peripheral vision for it to come back into view. You may also find with all this staring that you blink, and once you do the aura disappears. Blinking normally while attempting this maneuver is not something to be ashamed of. It has a way of resetting our conscious focus, so in the beginning the aura may disappear, but keep practicing and eventually blinking will not cause this to happen anymore. Seeing auras is not a skill that you can develop overnight. It requires a lot of practice and patience. A simple training exercise would be to tune in on some primary colors by focusing on some brightly colored objects. This exercise is most effective when performed in a softly lit room. By doing it the right way and for long enough, you should be able to see an aura emanating from the objects you are focusing on. Once you get the hang of it, there is no limit to how much you can vary your objects of interest.

Chapter 4: Advanced Techniques

Once you have a respectable grasp over the art of observing auras on inanimate objects or animals, it is time to raise the bar. It is advisable to start off by asking a friend of yours to help you out by sacrificing some of his or her time for you. Ask your buddy to stand with his or her back to a blank white wall in a softly lit room. Now try to attempt the same exercise that you tried for inanimate objects.

The key for a beginner practicing with a person is to not look the subject in the eye. This may cause you to lose focus. The aim here is to analyze the subject's aura. Make sure you maintain a steady gaze at the space surrounding the subject. It is rare that someone begins to perceive an aura immediately.

In such situations at least try to find a change in brightness in the space surrounding the person. The white wall behind the subject might appear to be a little dull as compared to the rest of the wall. Once you are able to perceive that change in the intensity of light the aura should not be too hard to see.

The next step after being able to see the color of the aura is to make sure that you do not lose it. Ask the person to move side to side and see if you are able to follow the aura's movement as well. Keeping the subject happy and energized helps to maintain a bright and steady aura. For those of you who have trouble acquiring a willing subject, you can always practice on yourself again.

Seat yourself in a softly lit room and relax. Focus on seeing your own aura. Rub your index fingers together till they seem adhesive. The aura is known to exude itself around places where there is a concentration of energy. One you feel that your fingers have become sticky, move them apart by a centimeter or so. Focus on that gap and see if you can make out smoke, fog or some colored mist in between the space of your fingers. With rigorous practice and hard work, watching an aura will become a lot easier.

Guidelines of 'Four'

Now that you have gotten the basics down and spent ample time practicing seeing auras readily from people and animals in any given moment, it will be helpful to know a few more things about auras to look out for. You should have gotten pretty good at seeing the transparent haziness just beyond the outline of people's bodies and your own. You should have also seen some color by now. Ideally, you would like to be able to have caught glimpses beyond the first physical level of the aura into the etheric and vital levels in order to move on to practice viewing the next properties of auras. If not, it is ok, be patient. Go back to the previous exercises and keep practicing until you get very comfortable with them. Otherwise you may become bothered with trying to grasp these advanced techniques to follow. Small steps lead to big rewards!

So then you know what auras are, what their colors are and what they mean, you know that the colors of a person's aura can change often, and you are aware of the seven layers of the aura body. But did you know that auras can vary in shape, size, position and type? These differences are helpful to be aware of when observing a person's aura and add to the characteristics of how auras are defined. Let's take a look.

Shape

The definition of your aura's shape depends on how you respond to the experiences you encounter in life. Remember that as people go through life they change, and their auras are no exception. The color of a person's aura can change, and so can their shape. These have to do with a person's sense of personal boundaries. Their appearance matches their name. There may be others, but listed here are the four most common ones seen:

Fuzzy

If you can guess, a fuzzy aura reveals a clouded sense of personal boundaries. This person is probably aloof and does not know how to establish themselves. They most likely have an underactive root chakra. The fuzzy aura indicates a tendency to take on and get caught up in other people's personal problems. It also points to the inability to neutrally say 'no' to others. It shows that this individual is a people-pleaser and believes setting personal boundaries will deter others from liking them.

Wall

A person with a wall-shaped aura is trying to define personal boundaries for themselves but doing so out of personal protection. The wall indicates defensiveness by being emotionally or mentally unavailable or both. It shows a tendency to assert one's determination by resistance and judgement. This person was most likely hurt or double crossed in the past and has yet to be able to recover, or does not know how to open themselves up emotionally.

Spiky

It is what it sounds like. The spiky aura is a passive aggressive or aggressive aggressive indicator of someone who feels like a constant victim and either assumes blame on themselves where it is not relevant or readily points blame to others. Spiky depicts feeling threatened and ready for conflict. It suggests that the person the aura belongs to is deeply wounded and has usually experienced some kind of abuse, whether it be physical, sexual, mental, emotional, or another. They are very reactive and will often hurt other people, even if they are trying to help.

Neutral

A person with a neutral aura has well-defined and

healthy boundaries with others. The oval or 'egg' shape of this aura exudes a sense self-understanding and responsibility for oneself. This balanced individual owns their space without having to fight or defend it. They can be free and easygoing or curt and to the point, but they know themselves well enough to respond without being emotionally charged or guarded; they are empowered to be neutral regardless of circumstance.

Size

The size of aura pertains to how a person exerts themselves and shares their personality. There may be other possible alternatives that the ones listed below, but these are the four most commonly defined patterns that are observed.

Large

Large and in charge is the theme of this one, although it does not necessarily allude to effectiveness. A large aura infers the intention of the individual to dominate or control others. They like to be in control of their surroundings and will therefore have an aura that is as far-reaching as possible. On the other hand, the expansion of a large aura can mean that a person is trying to be too responsible for others and results in them spreading themselves too thin. This aura size may be characteristic of micromanagers. Because this aura size is so big, the concentration of the energy field is diminished and it becomes easy for one to lose touch with their inner self, being too focused on things outside of oneself. Keep in mind though that highly spiritual people who walk the walk and ascended masters have an increased range in their spiritual prowess. So while these masters will have an aura size that is large too, the difference is that despite the size, the concentration of their energy field will be rich with a healthy glow.

Small

As you might imagine, a small aura size has characteristics that are opposite to those of someone with a large aura. They are withdrawn, meek, easily intimidated and experience a continuous feeling of fear on some level. The only way that this might change is by removing or growing beyond this fear. The person exuding this aura size or apparent lack thereof, since it remains closely drawn to the surface of the skin and inside the body, will most likely be introverted and hoping not to attract attention to themselves. There is a sense of holding back their energy until they feel safe. This withdrawal and containment of energy can cause constrictions within the body pertaining to blood vessels and energetic meridians, which lead to a number of health problems. One of these problems can be myofascial pain syndrome, which is the development of several knots in the muscles throughout the body, leaving the person feeling constantly stiff. It is easy to lose a sense of self with this aura size because the person is confining themselves without allowing an outlet to express who they really are.

Absent

This aura 'size' is characteristic of people who appear distant, removed, or otherwise "checked-out" from the present moment on a regular basis. They may be indifferent and incapable of making decisions, even simple ones. They may also have a severe type of depression in which they feel numb to the world. The absent aura refers to being unhappy with life or deeply wounded in some way and unconsciously avoiding any pain or facing any problems in life. This is possible as being a spirit out of body while still going through life, but it results in a lackluster sense of living as just going through the motions in every aspect. Eventually the person with an absent aura, which will be floating above their head instead of emanating around their body, will need to deal with these issues. You may have heard of people having "out of body" experiences, which are different in the case that it is ok to do this once in a while.

Healthy, Balanced

Just like it sounds, this is the typical aura size we have been referring to in this book. It has an egg shape and extends about three feet or an arm's length around the body. This healthy aura size promotes awareness of others and the surrounding world. It refers to a balanced sense of presence in the moment and allows for a regulated flow of energy.

Position

The position of a person's aura is probably the most mobile and temporary. These can change from moment to moment because they move depending on how a person is interacting with life. However, because aura positions primarily have to do with the mindset of the person, they can get stuck in a habitual mind frame and the prolonged state of an aura out of a centered position can result in postural issues. People generally favor one position over others by how they conduct themselves in accordance with the demands of daily life. For example if a person must take an exam but is procrastinating from studying and avoiding it at all costs, the position of their aura will move to float above the body. Once the exam is over though and the sense of need to escape is gone, their aura will move back into a centered position.

Front

This position is indicative of getting ahead of oneself, or leaping before they look. The person is looking into the future and may well only want to see what lies ahead without paying attention to their present reality, or feels so pressed by future demands that it is all they can think about and their aura moves to the front to lead them on. It can be the result of stress and anxiety, and with prolonged time spent in this position, the moved aura can also create stress and anxiety because the person is not fully enveloped by their energy field. An aura positioned in front of a person conveys that they are in a hurry. The habitual positioning of a front aura can eventually lead to postural problems such as kyphosis, which is the forward bend of the spine at the upper back, along with other health issues.

Back

A person who is dwelling on the past will find their aura at the back of themselves, behind the body. This is characteristic of people who have unhealed issues from the past or are constantly analyzing past events to gain some clarity of the present, or help plan better for the future, but they are immersed in this process. An aura positioned at the back of a person is also indicative of a fear of the future. The habitual positioning behind a person by dwelling on the past may prevent them from moving forward in life, result in depression, and also lead to postural problems like lordosis, which is the accentuated curvature of the spine going backward in the lower back.

Above

An aura floating above the body shares similar characteristics to the 'absent sized' aura in that they both portray the avoidance of facing realty, however an aura in the above position does not necessarily indicate listlessness or depression. Instead, it pertains to living in a fantasy world. People who talk a lot but do not have much to show for it will have an aura in this position. The concern with maintaining the above position is that it is often a result of some kind of trauma and can lead to further accidents, poor relationships, job loss, etc. if it remains there.

Centered

Just like the name states, a person who has an aura in the centered position is comfortable and makes a practice of staying present. They are fully enveloped in their aura in a balanced way. Keeping a consistency of being in this position is ideal and the desired norm. The centered position supports health, personal empowerment and having an aligned posture.

Type

The definitions of these auras come from a particular institute and field of study known as "Human Design." The originator of this system of learning and interpreting the nature of oneself, who is called Ra Uru Hu, has combined the corresponding systems of astrology, the I Ching, and the chakras and has built upon them in a very intricate way. There are many schools around the world that promote the teachings and understandings of Human Design. There also exist large manuals that one can purchase to learn all the inner workings of this system's charts and information so they can do readings for themselves and essentially for others as well. Uru Hu has also determined along with this system four particular types of auras, which are described in detail below, along with individual existential questions that help define them.

Manifestor

Aura: Closed/Repelling

Existential question: "Who do I impact?"

What this type means as "closed and repelling" refers to the idea that whenever a person with this proposed aura type interacts with another person, that other person's aura will be pushed back. This is a reason why life can appear particularly difficult for a person with a "manifestor" aura because they may see themselves as having a repelling personality without understanding why. The result of having this aura is getting a reaction from others that is not quite accurate. It does not mean that the "manifestor" type is unapproachable, it means that it is simply the nature of their aura and by this person becoming aware of this principle, they can relieve themselves of the sensation that something is wrong with them in a social dynamic.

Generator

Aura: Open/Enveloping

Existential question: "Who am I?"

This is said to be the most powerful of Human Design's aura types. People who have this type of aura are actually generating the life force of the planet. This is also believed to be the most common type of aura on the planet. These "generator" types will envelop another in their aura, which is very permeating. The "open" trait of this aura actually poses a vulnerability to the person with this type because by being open and enveloping, they take others' energies deeply into them for whomsoever they allow into their aura.

Projector

Aura: Focused/Absorbing

Existential question: "Who are you?"

While the first two auras of this system are considered to be "energy types" because they have the capacity to manifest and generate their own energy, this and the next aura type are classified as "non-energy types" because they are said to not generate their own energy, but instead must wait for another to generate some kind of energy in the form of an idea, action or conversation that they can then respond to. A person with a "projector" type of aura has a unique gift in that they are able to penetrate the aura of another in order to recognize them at their core being. Because a "projector" type remains so focused however, it means that they are vulnerable to conditioning while they are focusing. Another aspect of this type, in contrast to a "generator" type which is able to take in many others' auras at a time, or engage many people simultaneously, a "projector" is only able to take in one person at a time because of their "focused" nature.

Reflector

Aura: Resistant/Sampling

Existential question: "Who is different?"

This aura type is said to taste the world around them, "sampling" various aspects of their environment in order to discover what is out of place, what does not work, what is different, etc. The people with this type are looking for improvement in their world while remaining "resistant" to outside influences on themselves.

Benefits of Seeing Auras

- Smoke out liars: Auras are one hundred percent natural. They cannot be faked. Therefore, you can find out when people are being dishonest to you if you observe their thoughts. You will a notice a change in the quality of a person's aura as they are lying by the dimming or dulling of the intensity of the aura.
- Get insight into someone's nature: A bright, clear aura indicates spiritual advancement. A gray aura represents a person having unclear intentions or in ill health. A grey aura can also indicate that that person has a dark side to their personality regardless of how they present themselves at face value. A spiritual leader is always required to have a bright yellow aura around their head. In fact, if you are the type of person to seek out "masters," "spiritual teachers," or "gurus" to aid and guide you on your spiritual advancement, you will

definitely want to look for this characteristic in their aura. If he or she does not have it, you would be wise to consult elsewhere or seek within your own self. Otherwise you may become mislead.

- Diagnose diseases: Auras help to point out diseases and other physical, emotional and mental discomforts. Since it has been shown that information in the aura appears before it becomes evident in the body, you will be able to see these breakdowns before physical symptoms appear. By learning about your aura from sources such as this book and practicing to see your aura, you will be expanding your consciousness to learn how to control it as well. With that comes the ability to heal yourself.

Enhance personal growth: Observing auras raises the bar for your consciousness. It also assists in strengthening your awareness of the natural world, along with aiding spiritual development.

Chapter 5: Cleansing Your Aura

There are, in fact, many ways that an aura can be sullied. Remember that it is an electromagnetic field related not just to our spiritual bodies, but our mental, emotional, and physical bodies as well, so anything that can potentially weaken that will. That means inebriating substances like drugs and alcohol will put a damper on the brilliance of one's aura for the time that they are in a person's system and afterwards with any lasting side effects like dehydration and hang overs. The same goes for cigarette and other tobacco use. Sugars and especially refined sugars are like poison to a healthy body. They have a way of turning strong, flexible muscles and organs and sharp minds into gelatinous goo, so avoid them as much as possible. Stick to a healthy diet with plenty of vegetables like dark leafy greens (they contain lots of iron, good for blood circulation) and root vegetables along with fruits and good sources of protein. Water should also be a mainstay in your diet.

To illustrate a proper correlation of the function of our physical bodies, we can relate them to the power of a battery. Batteries maintain their power juices in an alkaline environment, and that is how we should look at keeping our bodies too. Many of the processed foods in grocery stores along with sugar, coffee and spicy foods turn the inside environment of our bodies highly acidic, which weakens it and thusly weakens our capacity to conserve, maintain and exert energy. Illness, harmful bacteria and cancer are allowed to thrive in an acidic environment while it has been proven that it is impossible for cancer to survive in an alkaline environment. If you feel your body may be too acidic, do some extensive research into a proper detox for yourself and consult your physician. Remember to always change your diet in gradual steps so that you may avoid harsh withdrawals get your body slowly used to the new changes; it makes the process so much easier and more enjoyable.

Some suggestions and home remedies are as follows:

- If you are a coffee drinker, work to limit yourself to one cup per day, and begin to substitute it for tea. There is a wide variety of teas out there, including black teas that taste earthy like coffee does, so you will be sure to find something that appeals to your tastes without having to endure the taxing effects.

- Replace sugar and artificial sweeteners with natural sweeteners like organic honey, stevia, or pure maple syrup. Maple syrup has been shown to have the lowest glycemic index (quantity of natural sugars), although if you go this route make sure that you are getting 100% maple syrup.

- Avoid spicy and greasy foods where possible. Of course it is fine to have them once in a while, but you want to have a balance suitable to your body's needs. If you have recurring indigestion or heartburn, this is a sign to consume them minimally.

- Excessive dairy products in your diet may be prevalent depending on who you are because diary is everywhere: milk, butter, cheese, sour cream, cream cheese, yogurt, creamer, ice cream, etc. The main thing to know here is that aside from certain disagreements with your digestive system, consumption of dairy promotes the increased production of mucus in your body that can cause congestion in your respiratory system and sinuses. This buildup dampens the energetic connectivity of your organs which depletes the strength of your overall energetic system, including your aura.

- The best and most stable way to alkalize your body is through eating vegetables. Root vegetables like sweet potatoes, turnips, parsnips, carrots, and beets will calm the acidic environment of your body.

- Another way to alkalize your body is to add one teaspoon of baking soda to 16 ounces of water and drink this daily. Be sure however to buy baking soda that does not have aluminum content in it, as this is harmful to your body.

- If you have a food processor, blend two cloves of garlic with an equal-sized portion of fresh ginger root, juice from a whole lemon and about a tablespoon of honey. Once all these ingredients are mixed, add 12 – 16 ounces of water and blend again, then pour into a glass and drink. It may not sound like the best tasting concoction, but the honey helps it taste like lemonade and the effects are well worth it. This elixir will act to remove built up plaque in your arteries that hardens them and constricts circulation, as well as help remove tar in the air passages of smokers.

Now that we have covered how to promote an optimal environment for you and your aura to feel best energized from a physical standpoint, let's take a look at the mental aspect of this next. Thinking negative thoughts bring the level of an aura's radiant frequency down, whether they are about ourselves, other people, or things in general. Negative thoughts cast into debilitating emotions such as hate, anger, resentment, jealousy, envy, guilt, and fear. Remember the experiments of Masaru Emoto with water and the corrosive effects negative thoughts have on water.

Train yourself to observe your thoughts and weed out

the negative ones. Every time you have a negative thought or feel doubt, catch it in the moment and transform it by replacing it with a positive one. Turn "I can't" into "I just don't know how yet" or even better, "I will give it my best" and mean it. As long as you do give it your best you cannot fail and you can confide in that because there is always practice that will make your best even better. By maintaining a positive attitude, you will learn to see the world differently, slowly but surely, to the point where you do not take on stress like you used to. By making your attitude less susceptible to stress, you strengthen your resolve, your sense of confidence, and thereby strengthen your energy field. You will notice it, and others will notice it too.

Now if you are thinking, "Is that it?" after reading that, you might have been expecting something a little more mysterious in regards to cleansing and protecting the aura. Well, that is not "it," but those are very basic components that shape the foundation for sustaining a healthy and powerful aura since you are coming to understand that everything is connected. Regular exercise that promotes healthy circulation, breathing exercises to increase nutritious, oxygen-rich blood for your cells, and stretching to promote clear pathways for blood and energy meridians are also foundational ways to sustain and strengthen your aura. Remember that grey or black spots in the aura point to health problems, so by maintaining a healthy body and mind you are effectively preventing those from showing up and keeping your natural energy field pristine.

It is an ancient Taoist understanding that the body must be healthy in order to provide the means for a healthy mind. A mind must be healthy in order to provide for a healthy spirit. We must listen to our spirit, our sense of awareness or our better and inner sense of knowing to guide our mind to allow us the most fruitful circumstances for fulling our desires in accordance with what is best for the spirit. In turn, we must allow our mind driven by our spirit to guide and govern what is best for our bodies so that we can manifest our dreams through action. This is a cyclical relationship that must be followed in such an order as to promote our best state of living.

Living in this world, we tend to pick up a lot of energy from the people around us. If we are going to be social, we have to understand that this is going to be the case, but it does not have to rule our lives. Some energies that we pick up from others are very good and can give cause for us to feel a sense of wonder or inspiration. Some of these energies may be negative and it may end up having a negative impact on our aura. All of us may have come across this experience but none of us might have paid any serious attention to it.

Sometimes, we might start off the day in a very nice mood. We might hang out with friends and generally have a good time. However, at some point of time you will start to realize that you are getting irritable and anxious. In some cases, it might go to the extreme of wrapping up a perfect day in an extremely bad mood. This might be an apt situation to cleanse or purify your tainted aura. Even if the situation is not as demanding or obvious, it is always a good idea to have a periodical cleansing. Your personal aura, no matter how clean, is likely to get tainted when you spend time in contact with other people.

Negative energy tends to spread and latch on to people fast. It is essential to get rid of this negative energy or convert it into a notable cause. A clean aura naturally puts a person into a good mood. It also helps the people around him or her to maintain a happy state.

It is all about the intermingling of energetic fields and influence of high and low vibrations that determines how we are affected, or perhaps how we allow ourselves to be affected. For example if you are confident in yourself and maintain a positive attitude and you happen to be in contact with a person who has a particularly negative outlook on live, always naysaying and criticizing, are you going to believe them and allow their outlook to change yours? Most likely you are not, so that person's negative, low vibrational way of being does not affect you: it passes right through you, just as how we spoke of denser matter like solids passing through more spacious matter like liquids and gases. And you have probably heard about the power of water, how it effortlessly moves around obstacles to continue on its path and over time begins to shape the solid environment it flows through that refuses to be moved. By maintaining a higher frequency for yourself, so too can you begin to shape the stubborn, close-minded nature of negative people.

Strengthen your mind by practicing positive thought and listening to your inner sense of knowing as to what is best for you. Be open to change as long as it has your best interests in mind. When we are unsure of ourselves or allow ourselves to act on the whim of others' negative influences, we are exposing our weak energetic field. This leaves us open to disruption and distortion in our own fields from others and we end up carrying it around with us.

By being around negative influences with a weak field, we fool ourselves into believing what they present as true and their toxic attitudes or behavior become our own – not just in the mind, but in the body too. When we are around physically sick people who are contagious, the reason that we may catch that sickness is because our own aura is weak. Our body becomes diluted to the influence of the sickness and copies it, making us sick too. A person who has a strong, harmonious auric field is much harder to distort. On the other hand, healthy individuals can help others to heal faster by radiating secure positive, clear information about the healthy accord of their bodies and minds; one's aura speaking to another's.

To clean your aura you can use the following meditation. It works extremely well for grounding and centering yourself while raising your vibration. Find a comfortable place to sit or lay down and close your eyes. Start by seeing, feeling, or sensing the bright golden light of the sun together with silver white light of the moon together above your head. Imagine these two weaving and intertwining together as they pour into the top of your head. As the mixture of golden and silver light fill your head and pour into your physical eyes and third eye, affirm to yourself that this will help you to see the truth and nothing but the truth. And then as it pours into your ears and inner ears, tell yourself that it will help you to hear the truth and nothing but the truth. As the rays of this light move down into your neck and throat, affirm to yourself that it will help you to speak only the truth.

Then allow this light to pour down over your shoulders, cleansing and invigorating every single cell as it touches them, going down your arms all the way to your fingertips and then back again into your chest. Any load you may have felt weighing on your heart is lifted up by this gold and silver light. Imagine it moving down into your abdomen and solar plexus, where it brings all your emotions into balance and harmony, also creating a perfect symbol of infinity where your diaphragm is. The light swirls and dances further down into your sacrum and your root at the hips and the base of your spine and then out the tailbone and into the earth. Go deep with this light, through all of the layers of the earth until you are at its very core, which you may call the god center of the earth.

From there, a beam of pure and radiant red light flows back up through the layers, carrying all the grounding and nurturing energies of Mother Earth with it. As this bright red light flows up through the layers it expands in great rings, carrying the magnetic properties of its mantle with it and reaching back up through the ground, pouring into your tailbone. Imagine this radiant red light filling and harmonizing every cell in your body, grounding you – your legs, your feet, your root and sacrum, all the way back up your abdomen into your chest, shoulders, arms, neck and head and back up through your crown where the silver and gold light of the moon and sun entered. Take a deep breath in and exhale, sitting with this feeling.

Imagine this light to extend all the way to your head from the feet like a blanket. Believe that this light has the power to heal and close up any holes in your aura. Hold that mental image for some time and believe in it. Also, imagine yourself to be surrounded by a blinding white light for maximum effect and protection.

Another technique to practice for cleansing and strengthening your aura is called the Violet Flame meditation. This involves closing your eyes and, starting from a ball of violet flame above your head, imagining being bathed in a bright violet colored flame that you should allow to play with and roll around all throughout your body. It helps to visualize this but it does not matter if you can actually see it or not. As it is spinning around in your physical body, ask it to pour out through you heart chakra and circle around the outside of your body so that is also cleansing your emotional, mental and spiritual bodies, as well as the seven layers of your aura. The most important aspect of using this meditation is to open yourself to actually feeling the invigoration that the Violet Flame provides. Feel the intention and the sincerity to transmute negative thoughts, emotions and anything that you wish to be changed or eliminated from your life.

Strengthening Your Aura

- Yogic cleansing bath: This is a special recipe that is used to strengthen your aura. It assists in detoxification from exposure to heavy metals found in tap water among other sources as well as radiation and removes blockages and distortions from the aura. It also helps to soothe itchy skin. This procedure has to be followed and repeated for seven days straight. It involves soaking in a tube of hot water for twenty minutes each day or until you feel dizzy or fried. The recipe calls for two cups and up to one pound of sea salts and two cups of baking soda. If you start to feel strange, the bath has done its job.
- Sage smudge stick: The North Americans consider the smoke from burning white sage to have cleansing properties. To get the cleansing effect, light a stick and allow the smoke to pass over your body. You can feel all your negativity being taken away by the smoke.
- The sun: Spending quality time in nature is always a healthy remedy to strengthen an aura. The sun loads you up with Vitamin D and lots of energy.
- Sea salt: A dip in the ocean or somebody of salty water has an energizing effect. It bolsters your

aura and increases its impact. A salt scrub before showering has a similar effect.

- Cold shower: cold showers are the perfect remedy for clearing away negativity and toxins. It is also known to release tension from the body and exponentially improve circulation. After a cold shower, your thoughts appear to be clearer and more collected. You become clear-headed and there is less confusion.

- Sound medicine: Sound has been accepted by many cultures as a healing tool. The "Om" chant is a classic technique to use and has seen a lot of centuries pass by. That chant has an extremely relaxing effect on the person. Recordings of Tibetan healing bowls and/or bells are also extremely therapeutic and effective.

- Avoid prolonged exposure to electronic gadgets: Modern day electronic gadgets are abuzz with radiation and multiple frequencies. There are electromagnetic frequency neutralizers that you can purchase as well. They come in the form of stickers as well as other devices that you can slap onto or put next to any electronic device and have been shown to absorb and neutralize the radiation coming off of it. Use your discretion though because there is a huge market for this type of thing and thus has attracted its fair share of fraudulent suppliers.

- Be aware of energy drainers: All around you there are people and situations that demand you to be mindful of your surroundings. Everybody is familiar with vampire culture. The lore began in Transylvania from a culture where people would hold a yearly celebration of slaughtering a family-owned pig and use every single part of it including the blood, which they would fry in a pan and spread on bread or drink straight up for its high iron and nutrient content much like eating liver. Nowadays vampire culture takes on a new meaning. It refers to those people who have such low vibrational energy fields that they prey on others whether they are aware of it or not to give them more energy and end up draining those others of their energy because they take without giving anything back. Keep in mind though that you can evade the effect these people and situations have by establishing healthy boundaries for yourself and keeping yourself at a high vibration. People who practice keeping high vibrational field are not easily swayed by energy vampires, they influence others to raise their own vibrational fields instead.

Violet flame meditation: Various sources are attributed to the origin of this meditation, one of them being St. Germain. Some people even say that Jesus Christ used this meditation during the years that he traveled and preached in order to maintain such a high vibration that he did.

Chapter 6: Protecting Your Aura

It is important to purify and maintain your aura. It is equally important to protect your aura from potential harm as you are working to increase and maintain a high vibrational energy field. The most popular methods to shield and strengthen your aura would be through heavenly intervention, massage and cord cutting.

Heavenly Intervention

It is believed that angels can help you preserve your energy from prying minds, assist in your power to heal, and provide protection for you in highly stressful or potentially dangerous situations. The catch is that the angels have to be called for help. They are celestial, omnipresent beings who are always at hand and ready to help, however, they have to be called upon before they can be of any service to you.

You may call on Archangel Michael in times of need for protection. He is associated with the color of light blue, so it would help to imagine a light blue mist surrounding you and flowing into your body through your breath when calling him. An invocation of Archangel Michael might go something like, "Dear Archangel Michael, I call upon you to assist in protecting me with..." or "I ask that Archangel Michael come to protect me and wrap me in his wings during this time of stress because..."

You can call upon Archangel Raphael when you require healing or wish for healing for someone else. He is connected to the color green, so envisioning yourself being surrounded in a shower of green light that penetrates through your body and all around is also helpful. You can ask Archangel Raphael to assist you in a way such as, "Archangel Raphael, I ask that you come to aid in healing..." or "Archangel Raphael, please bless my friend with your healing energy to relieve..."

When calling on the angels it is most helpful to be specific as possible when addressing the issue, but avoid being detailed as to how you might expect them to do it. Angels are very powerful, ever-present beings that work in wonderful ways we cannot understand in our present time with our level of consciousness. Once you have made your prayer, you can take solace in knowing that you have been heard and an answer will come to you. It may not come immediately, however it will come with the perfect timing. If you are still feeling uneasy about it, you can pray to them again and ask them to provide a sign for you. You will most likely find it in the strangest of places, and it might happen as one of those "too close to be coincidental" circumstances.

It would also be a good idea to read up on the particular angel you wish to call so that you can familiarize yourself with them and their attributes. Doreen Virtue is a wonderful author that has written a great deal about angels and how to bring them into your life. By getting to know the angels you are calling upon better, you are drawing them further into your consciousness which will create a stronger connection with them.

Massage Therapy

Massage works on cleansing and strengthening auras from a mostly physical standpoint. There are several benefits that come with getting a good massage other than just feeling relaxed. When the practice first began back in ancient Greece, it was considered a medical practice, and although the overall reputation of massage has unfortunately fluctuated throughout the years, it is still used as a medical practice today along with chiropractic practices and physical therapy.

There are different styles and techniques of massage that address various issues in the body. The primary of which is focused on promoting healthy blood circulation. When we forget to stimulate our bodies with physical activity and stretching, endure injuries related to muscle and tendon trauma, or partake in a diet of unhealthy foods, our circulation system becomes lethargic or constricted in certain areas. When this happens our muscles do not get the nourishment that blood provides them. The muscle cells are still engaged in metabolic activity, but the cellular waste that they produce gets backed up because the blood flow is not there or happening rapidly enough to remove those wastes. By this time, these backed up areas in the body begin to become toxic causing further health problems, including stiffer, more aggravated muscles. Massage works to resolve all of this by loosening up these stiff and constricted areas so that an abundant blood supply can get in to remove these wastes efficiently, and also encourage blood to flow more freely throughout the entire body.

Another facet of massage works with the lymphatic system, which is our body's natural drainage system for natural and unnatural wastes and toxins that are produced by and introduced to the body. When the lymphatic system gets backed up, the sacs that process these toxins, known as nodes, get swollen and we end up getting sick. If you have ever been to a doctor and remember them feeling around your neck underneath the jaw, they are checking for swollen lymph nodes. Regular massage assists with clearing this system out indirectly, but there is an additional technique known as lymphatic drainage massage that applies directly and consciously to assist in reducing the swelling of these backed up nodes so they may clear the toxins out of the body.

Massage therapists are healers, and in being so they are consciously applying their skills and positive intentions into helping you heal. So then, you are not just receiving a physical massage to aid in your relief and relaxation, you are also receiving the positive healing vibrations of their intentions as well. Furthermore, you may remember earlier in the book talking about how an aura can be diminished in certain areas or contain specific points that are gray or black and that these can be signs of ailments in the body. The areas of poor circulation, knots in certain places or traumatization in the muscles, and the buildup of toxins may all be factors corresponding to these signs in the aura that massage can address.

There is a little known phenomenon that can occur while receiving a massage known as a somatic emotional release. The term, beginning with "soma" which means "body," describes an event when somebody is touched in a certain place on their body and suddenly without that person's understanding why, they will burst into an uninhibited release of emotions, usually in the form of hysterical laughing or sobbing.

The explanation for this sometimes embarrassing but perfectly natural occurrence says that because we are composite beings of body, mind, emotion and spirit, and because everything that makes us up is intimately connected, our bodies have the capacity to store emotions. To put it more succinctly, our bodies can store emotional memory; remember how we talked about water before and the fact that our bodies are mainly composed of it? These stored emotions, often buried deep within us from traumatic experiences, which have yet to be released from our beings, are yet another example of distortions in the aura that can be cleared with the aid of massage therapy healing.

And then there is a different kind of massage that comes

from halfway around the world in relation to Westerners known as Shiatsu. You may be familiar with acupuncture: it is the science of manipulating a living organism's energetic system, comprised of meridians or energetic pathways that run throughout the entire body, to improve one's overall health via specific access points known as acupressure points, and these points are accessed with the use of needles. Shiatsu uses the same meridian system and acupressure points.

The difference is that the practice of Shiatsu employs the practitioner's fingers instead of needles to access the points. It also involves a number of really feel-good stretches that assist in opening up a person's energetic system for smooth flowing. If done right, Shiatsu can leave you with that same 'cloud nine' feeling that a good Swedish and Deep Tissue massage provides. It directly addresses our internal energetic system and any dysfunction therein that could be considered the gateway between the physical body and spiritual body. Since everything is connected, and can be even more aptly addressed by focusing on the higher vibrational bodies of energy in our system, a Shiatsu treatment can simultaneously address physical, mental, and emotional symptoms via the meridian system.

Knowing that principle makes Shiatsu a highly beneficial treatment for addressing illnesses of our total being more closely to the core issue. The problem with addressing physical symptoms of illness head on is that they are often not the root cause of the problem, so while a doctor may be treating and curing a certain symptom or group of symptoms, the main issue causing the symptoms is overlooked so it can potentially manifest in some other way or the symptoms come back later on. It is like pulling weeds out of a garden just below the surface of the soil so that they are not visible anymore, yet the root deeper underground that is causing the weeds to sprout still remains.

Underneath a physical symptom often lies the root of an emotional problem which puts taxing stress on the body or a mental problem because of a poor and resistant perspective that can manifest physical symptoms or perpetuate emotional problems that do the same. Sometimes even in karmic cases, a physical or mental illness will result due to a problem in a person's spiritual composition, which relates directly to the aura. These types of issues may find some relief of their symptoms from other methods of treatment that target the physical body like standard medicine or mental body like psychotherapy, but in order to be completely cured they require the intervention of a powerful spiritual healer.

Cord Cutting

Try visualizing a pod or a bubble of white light surrounding you. This light should envelope you like a shield of protection. It should have the power to repel all negative thoughts, psychic attacks or feelings. By practicing this visualization in meditation for 15 to 20 minutes a few times a day and daily, you conscious thoughts in this effort will strengthen the force of this field. A good energy shield can also prevent other people from siphoning your energy. During the course of the day, invisible cords of energy reach out from you and connect to the people closest to you. Positive energy cords connected to people like loved ones and family can never be severed or discontinued. However, those energy cords that propagate negative energy should be cut loose or it might deplete your energy source.

Skepticism

Sometimes people are able to see auras when they catch a migraine. People with a visual system disorder, epilepsy or a brain disorder are also able to perceive auras with relative ease. However, these auras are not similar to the ones encouraged by aura readers.

When aura readers claim to see colors emanating from a person who is made to stand against a blank wall, some scientists claim that it is not the aura that they are viewing. They argue that any visible color is only a product of retinal fatigue or other optical illusions such as humidity and temperature, much like mirages seen from heat waves in the desert. It is claimed to be far from psychic or supernatural powers.

Chapter 7: Auras in Healthcare

Aura healing is most popularly known as psychic healing, energy healing or spiritual healing. This method of healing is a reliable method to release unwanted energies and to remove unwanted energy. It also makes sure that any block that is preventing your energy from flowing is effectively neutralized. This enables our personal energy to get flowing, resulting in the natural healing of the physical, mental, and emotional bodies.

Rather than providing healthcare at the body level, aura healing deals with the spiritual energy system. The spiritual energy system consists of energy or meridian channels, auras and chakras. Most physical problems manifest as symptoms of a root cause, as we have discussed before. Physical problems are only a manifestation of energetic, psychic, emotional or spiritual causes.

Aura healing is most effective if the person believes in

self-healing. A typical aura healing sees a healer trying to support grounded people and trying to elicit a better flow of one's own energy. In spite of all this, these so-called healers cannot heal you by themselves alone. They require the patient to be a cooperative and willing participant who will not hinder the process. It is true, as we will see by example soon in the following section on Reiki, that a person's resistance to this kind of healing whether actively (consciously) or passively (subconsciously) reduces the effect of a spiritual healer's treatment for them.

At the beginning of this book we brought up the nature of light and its principle rule that it follows the path of least resistance. Now that you may understand when it comes to spiritual and energetic healing, the practitioner is actually making themselves a conduit through which they channel healing light from everywhere around them in the universe. It is not their own energy that they are intentionally concentrating into the ill person's body when it comes to practices like Reiki, it is the energy or light of the universe that is infinite which pours through them to where they direct it.

Think about it: if you understand concepts such as black being the absence of light and white being the collection of all colors in the light spectrum, why do you suppose illness appears as black and grey spots in an aura? When people receive a healing treatment to improve the quality of their aura, they are receiving pure white light, which holds the highest vibration in our known universe. Therefore if a person is not willing to receive treatment or agrees to participate but still *resists* the process by consciously or subconsciously holding onto some part of their illness they are not yet ready to let go of, the healing light that the practitioner channels will have a difficult time finding its way into this person's energy field to take effect.

In an aura healing, the first step would be to get oneself grounded and to identify the spirit in one's body. The healer then fine tunes your aura, guiding you to release unwanted energy through major energy channels. Another way it is done is by transmuting this unwanted energy with a positive, higher vibrational energy. Aura healing is also used to remove blocks and to create a flow of energy via the seven major chakras or energy centers. Healers can also be called upon to attend to specific health problems. A healing is considered complete when the healer helps you redefine the boundaries of your aura.

One of the most popular methods for energetic healing is through the practice of Reiki. This is a soft touch or no-touch therapy, depending on the receiver's preference. It helps to heal and seal your aura by channeling the influx of energy in the universe to remove, clear, or transmute blocked or stagnant chi.

A Reiki practitioner performs the role of a medium. He or she channels the divine energy in a very specific way through the hands so that it ends up in the personal energy field of the receiver where it is used to push right through blocked chi. This alleviates any emotional, mental, spiritual or physical dysfunction. The fascinating aspect about this practice is that the Reiki energy comes from a source of Higher Consciousness that knows where it is needed. So for beginner practitioners who are first getting a feel for Reiki, they do not have to know exactly where to administer the healing because the divine energy they are channeling will know where to go.

A Reiki healer can practice on themselves, other people, animals, plants, and even inanimate objects like crystals and disfunctioning electronic devices! Practicing on oneself is a good way to train. When a Reiki healer is developing his or her skills with consistent effort they are effectively raising their vibration, which results in more powerful healings. They are clearing out their own auras by focusing on opening up to the higher vibrations that are flowing through them in healing sessions. With this also comes a better sense of guidance to know where the divine energy may be most effectively directed when healing someone or something. Essentially, the healer is becoming more and more at one with this Higher Consciousness as they open themselves up further.

Because this energy comes from the natural universe and is divine in spirit, it causes no adverse effects. The only discomfort that may result from a Reiki healing is when the energy a healer has channeled knocks a stagnant emotional or mental block loose and reintroduces itself to the receiver's consciousness so that they may begin to deal with it in a way that lends to the healing process.

These blocks exist because the person has consciously or subconsciously repressed them earlier in their life, avoiding or ignoring them and hoping that they would go away as such. But obviously this is not how it works, so when a healing session breaks up a block, the person understandably gets upset at having to deal with it again, especially if it was locked away so deeply that they had forgotten about it or even scarier for them if they had never even realized it.

Taking this into respect, it is very important that a Reiki healer develop a very keen sensitivity to the people they are practicing on. They are directing influence, although positive, into some potentially very potent and traumatic issues, so they must learn to be gentle and very accommodating to the receiver with respect to how much that person can handle processing at the time. A really good Reiki practitioner will have developed this sense so they are open to receiving messages from that person's aura or the divine energy that they are channeling to be wise to these kinds of issues and handle them accordingly.

Because a Reiki practitioner is dealing directly with another person's aura, you would think that the ability to see it would come as part of the package; however this is not the case. A healer who practices Reiki may be able to see auras too, but that is dependent on their own natural abilities as a clairvoyant or the time they put in to develop the ability to see auras. Clairvoyants have been suggested to be visually sensitive and visual learners. Healers are suggested to be kinesthetically sensitive as well as learners. They learn best through their sense of touch, even if they are not physically touching anything, but energetically touching.

Another skill for Reiki practitioners to develop is the kinesthetic sensing of where a person's aura is. Is it protruding out far at their abdomen? Does it sink in close to their forehead? Does it spike or feel scrambled at the hip? Reiki practitioners use their hands to heal and to sense energy fluctuations, and the variations can be described as a pressure felt on the hand as it passes over part of person's body. The Reiki healer may also feel sensations like heat, cold, or tingling like pins and needles when a limb falls asleep.

Distance and Remote Healing
Spiritual energy is never limited by time or space. This paves the way for the success of distance and remote aura healing. Remote healing involves sending energy through time. It can be toward the past when a traumatic event occurred in a person's life for example. The energy sent will not change the event in history, but it will help to alleviate the pain or turmoil that the person experienced at that time and may very well be affecting them in the present. Remote healings can also be sent into the future. This can be done for a situation where a person can anticipate a stressful event because they know their own patterns well or someone else's.

If a person must give a speech in front of a huge audience in a week's time and they are aware that getting up in front of people makes them feel very nervous, they can request a remote healing. The practitioner will make the intention to send positive energy into the future at that time for the speech giver. When the time comes, the person giving the speech will feel not just calm but comfortable as themselves as if there was nothing to worry about in the first place.

Distance healing is notably useful when there are geographical or physical boundaries to overcome. If nothing else, distance healings help a person to relax and vent stress much more freely. They also have a revitalizing tendency that accelerates the recovery times for mental, physical, spiritual and emotional issues. Phone healings are also available.

In this type of healing you are guided to release any pent up negative energy. The whole process is facilitated through a phone call from the comfort of your own home. However, such levels of successful remote healings can be achieved only by experienced practitioners with a background of years dealing in energy work.

Auras and Chakras

- Root chakra: This chakra is located near the base of the spine. It is the center for information and energy in the entire body. The first chakra is directly associated with issues relating to organization, livelihood, work and money.

- Sacral chakra/Spleen chakra: The second chakra is located about four inches below the navel. This chakra is the center that relates to sexuality, creativity and clairsentience, also known as empathy, or the ability to sense other's internal feelings and emotions without those people expressing them. This chakra is also responsible for your sexual orientation, male/femaleness and sexual attraction standards. Therefore, when you are attracted to someone the second chakra spins like there is no tomorrow.

- Solar plexus chakra: the third chakra is located in the solar plexus, just below the ribs. It is considered the information center for energy distribution and personal empowerment. Most of the emotional blockages that impede an individual's progress are centered in the third chakra. This chakra is also responsible for your ability to read others' emotions while being the house of people's emotions. It also relates to the amount of energy you have at hand. Heart chakra: The fourth chakra is located right in the center of the chest area. It houses love, and your tendency to be at peace.

- Throat chakra: The fifth chakra, it is located at the base of the neck and throat. It is the center for self-expression and communication

- Third eye chakra: The sixth chakra is situated in the center of the forehead just above and between the eyebrows, and is thus also known as the brow chakra. It is the seat for clairvoyance, or clear sightedness in the form of intuition and inner vision.

- Crown chakra: The seventh chakra is located on top of the head at the crown. It is the center for spiritual information, as well as receiving spiritual messages and guidance. It is also responsible for inspiration.

A careful comparison between auras and chakras reveals that both of them have a lot of similarities. Each color in an aura pertains to a particular characteristic while each chakra has notable identities of its own. Both of these signals are used to identify and analyze various facets of human behavior.

Healing through Color

It has been common knowledge for a long time that color is part and parcel of a person's feelings and emotions. The study of color and healing is a lifelong pursuit. However, the most general guidelines are as follows.

Red

Red is commonly known as "The Great Energizer" and "The Father of Vitality". This color is warm and vital for heating. It relaxes stiffness and constrictions. Red also loosens or opens up clogs. Red is directly related to the root chakra. The color red has the effect of raising hemoglobin levels and body temperature. For this reason, it is often suggested for people suffering from anemia and other blood related conditions.

Orange

Orange has a very relieving effect on the body and the mind. As a mixture of yellow and red, it combines mental wisdom with physical energy. It induces a subtle yet important transformation between a higher mental response and a lower physical action. This is often regarded, "The Wisdom Ray". The color orange is warm and non-constricting. Orange helps to inspire new ideas and stimulates enlightenment. It links very profoundly with the sacral chakra. Therefore, it is very vital in dealing with sexual expression.

Yellow

This color helps to strengthen the mind and nerves. It stimulates higher mentality and inspiration. It is the color that should be used for nerve-related conditions. Yellow is always associated with the solar plexus. It is the psychic center of the body, sometimes referred to as the "seat of the soul." Consider that it is in the direct vicinity of the belly button, which was the vessel from which we all received our vital nutrients while in the womb. Yellow is also used to diagnose problems in the liver, stomach and intestines. It has a profound involvement in the healing of scarred tissues. It pushes the scarred tissue toward faster healing. It has a very profound effect on the brain and intellect.

Green

Contrary to popular belief, blue is not the color of healing. It is green. Green occupies the central position in the spectrum. Therefore, it is believed to have an equal balance or harmony. Green is the default color for healing. When in doubt, always use green. Every kind of healing uses green as a base. Therefore, you can never go wrong with green. It is the color of both the earth and nature. Green is associated with the heart chakra. Green directly influences blood pressure and so almost all prevalent conditions of the heart are associated in healing with this color.

Blue

Blue is the color that is best suited for the descriptions of being astringent, electric and cooling. It influences bleeding, fevers and sore throats. It is known to have a sedative effect. Blue is directly related to the throat chakra. It is referred to as "the center of power" and is sometimes regarded as the most important center in the body. It can also be used to resolve issues pertaining to speech and communication.

Indigo

Indigo is regarded as the official decontaminator of the bloodstream and is known to have a notable effect on mental health problems. It acts as a purifying and cleansing agent. Indigo is a blend of blue and red, with deeper accents in blue hues. It is directly associated with the brow chakra or the third eye chakra. It exercises control over the pituitary gland. It has some control over both the physical and spiritual perception. It is also used to assist in treatments related to the eyes and ears.

Violet

Violet is the color that has the most divine connection. It is not used much on physical levels. Some people believe that the color violet helps to revitalize the cells in the upper portion of the brain and has a connection with the crown chakra. Record states that Leonardo Da Vinci claimed of meditating under the influence of the inspiring rays of violet. This could explain why most churches have violet tainted windows.

White

As in aura reading and even in healing, white is considered the perfect color. It is the accumulation of all colors working and blending together harmoniously. It is the hue of the spirit that has awakened from slumber.

The above is just a brief summary of the roles played by colors in aura healing. In-depth learning and a complete understanding of the nuances of aura healing may take a lifetime. However, the points to be remembered by novice aura readers regarding healing is that complete healing is a function of some kind of internal transformation. This means that on some level in order to achieve a completely successful healing, the receiver should be willing to commit to some inner work on themselves to finish the process, or to realize that the process is complete. A healer can tell a person that they are already healed and they may as well be, but hat person must know it for themselves for the process to be finished.

Conclusion

I want to thank you once again for purchasing this book and hope that you found it interesting.

Reading auras is something that requires a lot of insight and patience. It cannot be mastered overnight and may not pass a reading test with a 100% result. The world's best aura reader is reported to have failed when subjected to a series of tests that were aimed at analyzing her abilities.

Similarly, aura healing is a very sensitive science. You cannot heal serious diseases by just looking at colors because this is far from possible. However, there have been instances where aura healing did help relieve and bring about some changes in a sick person. Aura healing is most effective when the healer has the complete cooperation of the patient.

So follow the guidelines extensively and you can use your Aura-sensing skills in the best manner. Good luck and enjoy.

<u>You May Enjoy My Other Books!</u>

<u>TAROT</u> : <u>Fortune Telling and Mind Reading Secrets</u>

<u>hyperurl.co/tarot</u>

MIND READING : Clairvoyance and Psychic Development

<u>hyperurl.co/mindreading</u>

<u>Chakra For Lovers</u>: Pleasure Guide Through Healing For Couples

<u>hyperurl.co/chakralovers</u>

RECOMMENDED READING

CHAKRA HEALING EXPOSED

smarturl.it/chakraaa

CRYSTAL HEALING ENERGY

smarturl.it/crystala

SUGAR: Shut Your Mouth To Sugar Addiction And Cravings Forever

hyperurl.co/sugar

HEARING GOD'S VOICE: How To Hear The Voice Of God

smarturl.it/heargod

SELF ESTEEM: Confidence Building: Overcome Fear, Stress and Anxiety: Self Help Guide

hyperurl.co/selfesteem

Made in the USA
Middletown, DE
07 February 2020